JUSTICE OF THE PEACE

F.B. MAY

P.O. Box 7774, North Augusta, SC 29841-7774

Prologue

This story is based on true events. Names have been changed to protect those still living and their heirs.

Christmas Day of 1921 was unseasonably warm at nearly seventy degrees Fahrenheit, even for eastern central Georgia No rain was in the near forecast. Still, it started out as a nice enough day. The only problem was the small rural community was not prepared for events which would take place. The families of Malcolm Wiggins and Reginald Smith would be altered forever.

Acknowledgements

I would like to thank my special friend, Michelle Bouchard, for the encouragement she gave along the way. Thanks to my sisters, Carolyn and Barbara, for giving me feedback. Much thanks to my friend, Judge David Roper, Senior Superior Court Judge of Richmond County, Georgia for his legal expertise.

CHAPTER 1

Reginald Smith was already issuing orders.
Reginald – or, Reg, as his friends called him – was
both popular and unpopular. Perhaps a better way of
phrasing it was you either liked him or you didn't. It
was one way or the other, no in between. That's how
he saw life – black or white, no gray in the middle.
At least, when it suited him best. And Reginald Smith
always did what suited him.

On this day, Reginald stood outside his
unpretentious farmhouse, arms akimbo and looking to
the east as the brilliant arcs of red, orange, and yellow
of the sun shone to mark the beginning of a new day.
He had a lot to take care of today. A lot on his mind,
he thought, that he would have to tackle one thing at a
time. One would think he would be inside making
merry on this Christmas Day. But Christmas Day
was just like any other day to Reginald. He was
Baptist by birth but had no firm beliefs in anything he

could not hold in his hands. He had no affinity for taking days off. You never made money if you took time off and he did enjoy making money. He had proved himself capable of that time and again. Reginald took things in life as he desired and used whatever – or whomever – he desired to the best advantage for himself. Oh, he was careful to be civil and courteous; however, he could be angered easily particularly when he was under stress. Reginald was a moderately wealthy landowner and had worked to get himself elected a justice of the peace. He enjoyed the work of being a justice. It didn't interfere with his farming and he kind of liked hearing the different cases that came before him. It helped with social standing as well. Social standing was another thing that came with being moderately wealthy. Of course, he wasn't as rich as some, but he could take care of his own and then some. Reginald had some thoughts along those lines today, taking care of his own.

First things first. While his lovely wife, Charlotte, was making breakfast, he would send over a couple of his hired hands to check on something for him, then decide what to do about the situation. That situation had rankled him for far too long and he wanted it resolved today. He walked over to the small wooden shack that was about 200 yards from his house. He knocked once on the door and turned the knob. It opened freely, just as he freely walked in after that one knock. He gave the occupants notice he was about to enter. It was his property, and he could do as he liked on his property. After all, he treated them well. They weren't slaves as in his daddy's day.

"Morning, Tiny," Reginald nodded to the tall black man standing at the kitchen water basin. The basin was as big around as a huge pumpkin, with long wooden planks held together tight by two iron bands that spanned the circumference of the basin. He knew this was Tiny's and Millie's water basin for drinking and for dipping out water for cooking. The second basin they called a tub, was larger and shorter, set aside on the kitchen floor and used for the weekly baths.

Tiny turned around quickly for such a large man, then replaced the silver dipper he had used to scoop up the water he had just drank. His large dark eyes were startled at first, but quickly showed no emotion at all. Tiny knew Reginald could come in at any time, but it always startled him and, if he were honest with himself, it made him angry. Best not to show that anger, though. It had not been that long ago that Mr. Reginald finally got it through his head that his black farm hands were not slaves.

"Yes, sir?" Tiny asked. Thankfully, Millie was in the bedroom making the bed. It rattled her when Reginald came in with only a knock.

"Tiny, I'd like you to go over and see if we can get down the road today," Reginald said, looking straight at Tiny. He had no interest in Millie or the rest of the house the two shared.

"A'right, sir," Tiny answered. "That be the Wiggins place?"

Reginald nodded, hands on hips. "Yeah. Take Peanut with you. You can take the horses and buckboard."

"I'll go right after breakfast, if'n that be okay," Tiny said.

Reginald's eyebrows came closer together as he said, "No, that is not alright. I need you to go now."

"Yes, sir," Tiny agreed hastily. It was Christmas Day and he did not want anything to ruin it for him and Millie. Reginald nodded curtly and left the small house. Tiny knew something was up.

Well, he would get to it and be back soon enough. "Millie, I'm gwine to the Wiggins place to check on the road for the Mister. Peanut's gwine with me."

Millie came out from the bedroom. "I heard. What's goin' on with that, Tiny?"

"Don't know rightly, but it's on the Mister's mind. I'll be back d'rectly." He kissed her and left to find his friend, Peanut.

Peanut – called such because of the way the top of his head was shaped – was in his own small house, celebrating Christmas with his family. While Tiny and Millie had no children, Peanut and Sally had four. Now the children, aged two through ten, were playing with the single toy they received for Christmas. The wooden wagon Peanut had built for them was sturdy. He had sanded it so no splinters would prick little fingers or toes and the children were gleefully pulling each other around in the back yard. Sally, a small black woman with bright, observant eyes, was preparing the special noon meal and did not want Peanut to leave her on Christmas morning to go on an errand, but what could she say? So, she kissed him and went back to cooking, watching her little brood from the kitchen window as they played in the little patch of yard.

Reginald, his slight frame showing the years of hard work, went back toward the wooden house he had built years ago. Walking up the steps he thought again about how he really should paint the house for Charlotte. Charlotte had born him eight children and had put up with quite a lot from him. In his own way he loved her – but he loved another, too. His other love had born him two children. Charlotte knew Sarah and had finally accepted the fact that Reginald had another family. Shaking his head slightly as if to shake away unbidden thoughts, Reginald went into the kitchen. His son, Milo, was eighteen now and a tall, strong young man. Milo was snitching one of the biscuits Charlotte had just pulled from the oven. Reginald smiled slightly as Milo walked quickly away to keep his hands from being smacked with Charlotte's dishtowel.

"Would you like something to eat, Reginald?" Charlotte asked, deftly handling a hot pan of fatback and stirring the grits. Eggs were waiting to be fried. Then she would have to put the finishing touches on the Christmas dinner. Supper would be leftovers.

"Well, yeah. I always eat breakfast, don't I?" Reginald answered his wife sharply. He didn't see her blink her eyes and pull back a bit as he pulled out the wooden chair to sit at the round wooden table he had built.

"Well, here you go." Charlotte had fried the eggs just the way Reginald liked them and placed them on the plate. A fork was the only utensil in use. Charlotte had long since given up on trying to make Reginald and her brood "act civilized". Only what was necessary was what Reginald Smith wanted and felt was due anyone. "Milo! Penny! Jeremiah! Thomas! Minerva! Y'all come on and eat!"

Milo came in from the living room and sat at the wooden table. His dark brown hair stuck up in a couple places. Reginald looked at his son, really looked at him, and saw a tall lanky young man with many years ahead of him. Milo made room for his sister, Penny, who came into the dining room, wheeling herself in her wheelchair. Penny had contracted polio when she was younger and now, a lovely young teenager, had resigned her fate to be in the wheelchair or on crutches for the rest of her life. She had the same brown hair as Milo, but it was long, and she wore it pulled back at the nape of her neck. She was a year younger than Milo and the two were close. She knew no one would dare make fun of her or harm her within yelling distance of Milo.

Jeremiah and Minerva came in shortly, looking as though they had gotten right out of bed. To be thirteen and seven, those two were an awful lot alike.

Thomas was the straggler who seemed to irritate his father the most. Of course, in his mother's eyes, Thomas could do little wrong. Sometimes Thomas just felt like he was the odd one out and could never do anything right for his father.

"Say grace," Charlotte reminded them. Reginald went through the motions for her sake, but the children made more of an effort to remember to thank the good Lord for their food.

Passing the grits and eggs to each other – except for Reginald, who had his plate placed in front of him - along with biscuits, fatback and syrup, the children listened as the adults spoke. It was not permitted for the children to speak at the table unless spoken to.

"Reginald, do you think we'll open the gifts after breakfast?" Charlotte asked with a twinkle in her eyes. The children's faces were so hopeful. Reginald looked up and around the table for a brief moment then back down at his food.

"I s'pose we can do that," he answered shortly. The children had been holding their collective breath and now slowly released it. They *did* have a present! "But after that I want Milo to go with me for a drive."

Charlotte and Milo looked at each other, then at Reginald, whose blue eyes were cast down. "But, it's Christmas Day, Reginald. I thought we'd spend the day together with the children."

Reginald looked at her with finality. "It won't take long for what I need to do. Besides, the young'uns won't miss us for a couple hours." He determinedly looked away from the disapproval in his wife's eyes. She had a feeling, a gut feeling, that something bad was going to happen. She just didn't know what.

"Do you have to take Milo?" she asked.

"Yes! I need Milo! Now that's the end of it!" Reginald shouted. Charlotte and the children got very quiet and an uneasy feeling crept over the household. They had endured this feeling many times, but not so much on Christmas Day. Charlotte got up and went into the kitchen to tidy up.

After breakfast, Reginald followed through on his promise to open the gifts. Each child was delighted with a doll or toy that was carefully chosen for them by Charlotte. The best part, though, was the special delights: fruit, nuts, and candy. This was the only time of year they were allowed these scrumptious delights. After having his share, Milo hugged Charlotte and went outside to join Reginald.

"Where we goin', Papa?" Milo asked eagerly. At that moment, Tiny and Peanut came into the yard in the buckboard.

"Well?" Reginald asked them.

"The gate is still closed, and Mr. Wiggins be on the porch," Tiny told him, reins still in hand.

"Alright," Reginald said dismissively. He turned to Milo, allowing Tiny and Peanut to put the horse and buckboard back in the barn. From there they gratefully returned to their homes and had breakfast with their families, happy to leave Reginald's dealings to him and his boy.

"We're gonna go pick up Barry and Michael, then head out to check on the roads," Reginald said looking toward the east as they walked.

"I'll hitch up the buckboard?" Milo offered, about to veer off toward the barn.

"No," Reginald answered. "We're taking the car today." He glanced at his son, his expression confused and happy. "And you can drive." Milo was ecstatic! He enjoyed feeling the rush of the wind in his hair and the way the car speeded along the roadways. And *he* was driving the car that would pick up his cousins. He could hardly wait to see their faces.

In the doorway, Charlotte watched the car pulling out of the yard and onto the road. No, today was not going to be a good day after all. She could feel it.

Milo was extremely happy to be pulling the Model T into the dirt yard of his cousins, Barry and Michael. Milo and Reginald found the brothers near the chicken coop, repairing the latch. They looked around to see who was coming into the yard and broke into wide grins. Barry let his hammer fall to the ground and Michael rested his arm on the top of the coop door and waited for their uncle and cousin to come over to them.

"Morning, Uncle Reginald," said Michael. Barry nodded his recognition with a smile and nod.

"Morning, boys," Reginald said as he and Milo approached. Milo nodded his head at the two.

"What brings you here today, Uncle Reginald?" Barry asked. "I thought you'd be celebratin' like Daddy's doing. "

Reginald knew exactly how their Daddy, Buck Jenkins would be celebrating Christmas Day. He would be drinking and sweet talking his wife, Reginald's sister, into all sorts of things. For all his brother-in-law's faults, he did love Reginald's sister, Mary. It was just the three of them, the Smith siblings: Mary, who was the baby, then Reginald and Clayton, who were identical twins.

"Well, I thought I'd ride over to talk with Malcolm. See if I can talk some sense into him."

The young men looked at each other a bit uneasily. They knew of the feud that had been going on for nearly a year now between Reginald and Malcolm. It was enough knowledge to give them pause.

"Well," Michael answered. "If Mama and Daddy don't mind, we'll be glad to ride with you."

"Good," Reginald nodded. "Go on and ask 'em."

"Come on in and say hey to them, Uncle Reginald," Barry said encouragingly. "You know Mama wouldn't want you to go without saying hello to her."

Reginald shrugged a bit and followed the boys into the wooden house. It was slightly larger than Reginald's and clean as a whistle, just like Charlotte kept their own house. Reginald took off his hat when he walked inside and met his sister coming from the kitchen.

"Reginald!" she exclaimed with a smile, arms outstretched. "So nice to see you today."

Reginald hugged Mary and looked at her. It still amazed him that their sister could tell him and Clayton apart when most people couldn't. Mary was shorter than her brothers and had slightly lighter hair than they did. She wore her long dark hair in a bun at the nape of her slim neck. She, like her brothers, had inherited a slight frame. Her heart shaped face was still pretty, with blue eyes shining. Yes, Mary seemed happy and at peace with the world. She always did have a sunny disposition. Clayton had a good bit of that, too, but Reginald had turned out to be the sour one of the bunch.

"Come on in and sit a spell," Mary offered. Then her eyes fell on Milo, and she smiled wide.

"Well, Milo Smith! I swear you have grown another two inches if one." Milo smiled sheepishly, liking the compliment very much. He had a soft spot for his Aunt Mary. She was always considerate of everyone, and he knew she loved her nieces and nephews fiercely.

"No," Reginald answered, looking at the floor then at his sister. "We've got to be going. Thought I'd let Milo drive the boys and me up the road by Malcom's place."

Mary's smile faded as she glanced from Reginald to Buck and then to the four young men.

"Today, Reginald? Christmas Day?"

"Sure," Reginald said, not quite meeting her eyes. "It's just a drive and I wanted to see if Malcom has the gate open. We'll be back d'rectly."

Mary swallowed. "If it's alright with Buck, then, sure." Buck nodded at Mary. "But be back soon."

"We will." Reginald hugged Mary and nodded to Buck before he went out the front door. Mary gave Reginald a sharp look. The look conveyed her meaning well – do not get into trouble.

Milo hopped into the driver's seat and smiled at Michael. "Hey, Michael, would you mind cranking her?"

Michael walked over to the Model-T and turned the crank. He knew to expect a kickback from the crank, so he was ready when the inevitable backwards motion happened. The motor sputtered once then began to hum. He jumped into the back seat. Barry gave his brother a look and relayed a meaning to him without speaking. Looking down at the floorboard, Michael saw what his brother had already seen. There on the floorboard were three rifles. The two looked at each other, then at their uncle. They shrugged their shoulders slightly and determined to enjoy the ride instead of thinking of what might happen. Milo was a good driver, so Reginald did not worry about the driving aspect of their short trip. Milo carefully drove out of the yard and onto the dirt road. A mile or so further he turned down the next dirt road, went about another mile and drove slowly past a white clapboard house with a rather small front porch, set off the road about five hundred feet. There was a dirt driveway that led past the house to the red barn behind the house. Reginald attempted to show he was just out for a drive with the boys; yet he couldn't help but look at the house. On the porch was Malcolm Wiggins, standing tall and holding a shotgun.

Milo drove as far as the large wooden gate would allow him. It was located about two hundred yards past Malcolm's house. Upon seeing the gate still there with its crisscrossed boards to give it stability, along with the large padlock on the chain, Reginald slammed his hand on the dashboard of the car.

"Dammit!" he snarled. "When is Malcolm ever goin' to come to his senses about this here gate?" He turned his head back around toward the Wiggins house. "Turn around and drive slow by the house, Milo."

Sensing a growing tension and being uneasy, Milo did as he was told but said, "Papa, you okay?"

Reginald did not answer. Instead, he picked up his 12-gauge shotgun and put the shells in it. "I'm right as rain, Milo," Reginald answered without taking his eyes off the house coming up in his vision. The boys in the back seat looked uneasily at each other and back to the house with the man standing on its porch.

Malcolm Wiggins was of medium height with brown hair. He looked shorter from the distance of the motor car, standing with his legs apart, a defiant stance, with his shotgun in his hands. His bright blue eyes took in Reginald and the young boys with him. He knew this morning that a confrontation was coming. That was the reason for sending Abigail and the girls to Abigail's parents' home for Christmas morning. They had not wanted to leave, but he had insisted after seeing two of Reginald' hired hands on the horse and buckboard this morning. Now he was glad he had made that decision. He would defend his position until the death if it came to that.

Reginald told Milo to go as slow as possible now, without choking down the motor car. He yelled out to Malcolm. "Malcolm! Why don't we act like neighbors, and you take down that fence? You know I need to get to the creek."

"You can go around the long way, Reginald!" Malcolm shouted back. "The state says I'm in the right with my fence just the way it is."

Reginald became very angry. He lifted his gun to Malcolm. In that moment Malcolm saw his action, most likely believing it to be a threat, and fired his shotgun at Reginald. Reginald was startled for a few seconds. He didn't think Malcolm had it in him to actually shoot at him. But because he had, Reginald returned fire. "Help me out, boys!" Reginald shouted to his son and nephews. Obediently, Milo swung the car around while the nephews took up the rifles from the floorboard. They checked for ammunition, suspecting the rifles were already loaded, and opened fire at the man standing on the porch. There was gunfire for several minutes. When all was said and done, Malcolm Wiggins lay dead on the front porch of his home, riddled with double ought buckshot and bullets. Reginald and Milo were shot, as was Michael. Barry was the only two who remained physically unscathed. Emotionally and mentally, though, he would never forget this day.

Reginald got out of the car and limped to the front porch of Malcolm's home. He sat down beside Malcolm, shaking his head. "I'm sorry, Malcolm. I didn't mean for it to come to this." He slowly closed Malcolm's blue eyes for the last time.

"Milo, you alright?" Reginald asked his son who was standing by the car. It was then that he noticed the car had several holes in it where Malcolm had shot at them.

"I'll get by," Milo breathed hard, holding his side. Blood oozed through his shirt and Reginald's heart tightened.

"Milo! You're hurt!" Then Reginald had the sense to look around to see if anyone else was injured. "Michael! You're bleedin', too!"

Michael cradled his left arm as he spoke to his uncle. "I'll be fine, Uncle Reginald. Just a little wound. Smarts a bit, though."

Thank God Barry was not injured as well! Mary would have his hide as it was. Then Charlotte would take over.

"Boys, we've got to get the sheriff and the doctor," Reginald told them. "I'll drive."

The drive down the dirt road was rough, but at least it was level. That meant Reginald did not have to turn around and drive up an incline backwards before he got to a place where he could turn around. What was Henry Ford thinking, grimaced Reginald, when he put the gasoline tank under the driver's seat? Finally, he turned onto the highway leading into Millen. Millen was a tiny town situated between

Sardis and Statesboro. The six miles seemed like sixty to him right now. Reginald knew what he had to do. Beside him, Milo held his chest and leg, staunching the bleeding the best he could. In the back seat, Michael and Barry were white-faced. Michael's arm was not bleeding as much as it had been, but he was in pain. Reginald eased the Model T into the area of the sheriff's building, got out and as he shut the door looked at the young men.

"Now, boys," he said in a grave voice. "I don't want you to say a word unless I nod to you. Understand?" All three heads nodded affirmatively. Reginald went around and opened the car door for Milo, allowing Barry and Michael to climb out after him. They all walked into the building, limping, and bleeding or holding on to one another.

CHAPTER 2

Reginald had been furiously thinking while driving to the sheriff's office. Those six miles were some of the longest he had ever traveled. Why had he been so insistent on today of all days? He dreaded – purely dreaded – telling Mary and Charlotte what had happened. Reginald was not sure they would ever forgive him.

He thought of his son, Milo, sitting quietly beside him, biting back the pain. He had put pressure on the wounds and had acted like a man. In some part of Reginald's brain, he registered this and was proud of Milo. But he was also afraid for him. In the back seat, Barry had sat close to Michael who had been holding his bleeding right arm. No one had said anything on the drive in. Eventually Reginald had pulled the car in front of the sheriff's office. After pulling up the hand brake, he had jumped out of the car and raced around to Milo. He yanked open the car door, carefully lifted Milo, and half carried him into the Sheriff's office.

The Sheriff's office was already sixteen years old, yet the red brick building still looked newly built and boasted four cells in the back. Reginald had been here many times in his role as Justice of the Peace and as a friend to the sheriff. Now his hands trembled as he brought his son in, helping him sit in a chair. He was vaguely aware of his nephews coming inside the Sheriff's office as Deputy Mark Sanders came running around to see what was going on. Deputy Sanders stopped suddenly as he took one look at Reginald's grimaced face and immediately turned to the Sheriff's office door.

"Sheriff! Sheriff, come quick!", Deputy Sanders yelled, then turned back to the now four men in the lobby.

Reginald furrowed his brows and barked out, "Git me something to stop this bleeding!"

Deputy Sanders hurried to the bin where towels, washcloths, and strips of cloth were kept. He grabbed three towels, hurried back and gave two of the towels to Reginald and one to Barry to place on Michael's arm. Sheriff Abram Wilson came running into the room and skidded to a halt.

"My God, Reginald! What happened?" Sheriff Wilson asked incredulously. Before hearing Reginald's answer, he turned to Deputy Sanders. "Mark, get the doc!"

"Yes, sir!" And with that, Deputy Sanders was calling the doctor's house.

Sheriff Wilson helped Reginald lay Milo on the bench that was placed across from the Deputy's desk.

"Abram," Reginald began. "I went over to Malcolm's place this morning. He's dead."

Sheriff Wilson looked warily at Reginald. "Malcolm's dead? What happened?"

"I shot him." Reginald looked at the sheriff fully.

Sheriff Wilson stood up slowly as did Reginald. They looked at each other a moment longer, the sheriff trying to digest the information and decide how to handle this mess. He liked both Reginald and Malcolm and had known of the feud between the two men since the highway department had closed the small road running by Malcolm's home. It had effectively made a hardship on Reginald's ability to take care of his farming, for now he had to go around the new road and through the back way to get to the water needed. But he hadn't expected this outcome.

Sheriff Wilson looked at Milo, Barry and Michael. He surmised who had been with him, particularly since Michael, Milo and Reginald were bleeding. Reginald followed the sheriff's gaze and finally looked at his own leg. The blood ran down in small rivulets from a moderate sized wound. The fabric of his pants was burnt where the bullet had entered, where it remained.

The door of the sheriff's office opened and Doc Martin waked in, carrying his black satchel. He took one look around, set his satchel on the deputy's desk and rolled up his sleeves. Doctor Charles Martin had treated most of the people in Millen and Jenkins County, as the new county was called. It had been formed in 1905 from a little land that had each belonged to Burke County, Emanuel County, Bulloch County and Screven County. Doc's demeanor was a little brusque, but people quickly warmed up to him.

"Merry Christmas to y'all, too," the doctor said dryly. "Deputy, I'll need some hot water and towels."

Deputy Sanders had been anticipating the doctor's needs and had the kettle on and more towels out. "Comin' up, Doc."

"Wanta tell me what happened, Reginald?" the doctor asked as he bent down to examine Reginald's leg.

"Take care of the boys first, Charles," Reginald said. He motioned to Michael and Milo.

"Well, their wounds will hold for now. Yours may not," Doc Martin answered while taking some scissors to cut Reginald's pant leg. "Sit down."

Deputy Sanders had poured the hot water into a basin along with some cold water and brought it, along with the towels, to Doc Martin. He stepped back and watched as the doctor tended to Reginald.

As the skilled doctor had done for nearly thirty years in this community, he talked as he worked. Cutting the left pant leg up to the thigh, he peeled the fabric back to reveal rivulets of blood coming from a large hole in the front thigh.

"Well, think you can bear it while I take out the buckshot?" he asked Reginald.

"Of course," Reginald answered. He looked less sure than he tried to convey. Biting down on a bit of leather, sweat popped out on his forehead as the doctor began picking out pieces of buckshot – one by one.

Back at the Smith home, Charlotte was restless. The youngest children were playing outside together with their toys and squealing with glee. They played with Peanut and Sally's children. The children began sharing their toys with each other, basking in the day to rest, eat as much as they wanted, and play to their hearts' content. Tomorrow they would begin the grueling chores again. The older children were taking a well-deserved break from the back-breaking chores that came along with farm life. Charlotte tried to sit in her rocking chair but couldn't settle. So, she pushed herself up, walked to the kitchen and pulled out the utensils needed to make a cake. She did this effortlessly as Charlotte knew exactly where everything was in her large kitchen. That was the one thing she had insisted on when Reginald had built the house – a large kitchen and eating area. He had given her that.

Getting out the flour from the wooden barrel, she carefully sifted it into the bowl. Where was Reginald? He should have been back by now. The lines on her forehead furrowed as she cracked three eggs into the mixture and began to beat the contents together. Holding the bowl up near her chest, stirring vigorously and a couple strands of hair waving slightly is how Reginald saw her when he and Milo came into the kitchen. Then he heard the sound of the bowl breaking.

CHAPTER 3

Charlotte had been stirring together the ingredients to make a cake when Reginald and Milo walked in. She looked up, relieved they had returned. Her relief was short-lived. She saw first Reginald's grimaced face and that he was helping Milo to the couch. They were both bloodied and exhausted. The bowl slipped from her hands, crashing onto the floor as her hands flew to her mouth. It took Charlotte a few seconds to comprehend what state they were in, but when she did it took half that time to step into action.

"My mercy, Reginald! What happened?" she asked loudly. She quickly helped her husband get their son onto the couch and put pillows under his head. Scanning the length of his body, Charlotte took in the holes in his clothes and the caked blood on his hands and face. Then, looking up at Reginald, she saw blood on him as well as holes in his clothes, too.

"Reginald, what happened? Are you hurt?" Charlotte asked breathlessly.

"Mama," Milo whispered. "I'll be alright."

"Hush, now," she gently admonished Milo. "Let your daddy speak."

Reginald straightened up, his soreness and weariness evident. "You better sit down, Charlotte." She sat in the rocking chair and waited. Reginald sat beside her in his rocking chair, stretching out his injured leg. He took a deep breath, wincing as he did, and began.

"Milo and I stopped by Mary's place and picked up Michael and Barry. Milo was driving, which, as you know, he likes a lot. He did good, too," Reginald praised his son, giving him an encouraging nod. Charlotte's jaw moved in the attempt to not shout at her husband. But she said, "Go on."

"Well," Reginald continued. "We rode out to Malcolm's place to check on the road."

Charlotte closed her eyes tight, then opened them again. "Today? You went there today?"

Reginald squirmed a bit but answered her gruffly. "Now don't start, Charlotte. Just listen." He waited a breath to make sure his determined wife would comply. "Well, as we were going by his place, he was standing on the porch with his shotgun in his hands. That wasn't what I wanted to see. Especially today," he added quickly, looking up at her. Her mouth was in a firm line, which did not bode well for him, he knew.

Then his eyes took on a faraway look, as though he was right there again. "When we got right in front of his house, Malcolm just hauled off and started shootin'." Looking a little bewildered, Reginald continued. "'Course, I had to protect myself and the boys, so I took out my shotgun and returned fire."

Charlotte's left hand flew to her mouth. She began to slowly shake her head as he continued his recount of the incident.

"One of his shots hit Michael in the left arm. He's okay," he added quickly noticing Charlotte's quick intake of air. "Doc took care of the wound for now and he'll be just fine." Seeing his wife relax just a little, he continued. "Barry's okay. He didn't get hit. When Milo turned the car around and drove back past the house, Malcolm," Reginald's voice cracked. Once he had regained his composure, he said, "Malcolm shot Milo in the side. Doc couldn't take the pellets out right now."

"Why not?" a frightened Charlotte asked

"Doc said the swelling needs to subside," answered Reginald.

"And you?" Charlotte asked, placing her hand on his arm.

"Doc was able to get the pellets out of me. I'm just sore but it'll heal soon."

As though shaking herself out of a fog, Charlotte asked the question he had dreaded. "What about Malcolm? How is he?"

Reginald bowed his head, shaking it slightly. "I shot him, Charlotte. I shot him dead."

Everything was quiet in the Smith house at that moment. Even the other children who were in their bedrooms seemed to sense all was not well. Charlotte's look of horror was palpable. Reginald felt bad about what he had done. Milo looked as though he would be sick.

Charlotte was the first to speak. "No! You didn't, Reginald! Tell me I'm hearing you wrong!" After a few seconds of no words coming from Reginald' mouth, she said, "I'm going over to Mary's and check on them. It's going to be hard for her and the boys." She had to be moving. Reginald knew the unspoken,

"It's going to be hard on us, too." He nodded. "I told Mary and Buck what happened." After making certain her son was as comfortable as she could make him, Charlotte gave a curt nod, wrapped her shawl about her shoulders and started out the door.

Her feet seemed to know the way to Mary's and Buck's house of their own volition. While she walked, Charlotte thought. Trying to keep her mind sane, she reviewed the events as Reginald had told them. In her mind's eye, she could she Malcolm and Abigail's house. The same style house as she and Reginald had. Six rooms constituted the house: a kitchen that included a dining room area, a parlor and four bedrooms. The houses were made of wood and clapboard siding. The outhouse stood around back. Straight down the road she walked until she reached their house. Stopping for only a moment, Charlotte took a deep breath and walked up to her sister-in-law's door.

Buck opened the door to allow Charlotte to enter. She offered him a hug, which he accepted, and nodded his head in the direction of the parlor. Walking slowly and breathing deeply, Charlotte saw her sister-in-law and best friend sitting on the couch looking off into space. She tentatively sat down next to her and placed her hand over Mary's. Mary looked up and tried to smile but burst into tears. Charlotte wrapped her arms around her friend's shoulders and hugged her, letting her own tears fall.

"Mary, I'm -," Charlotte began, but Mary put her hand up indicating quiet.

"No, Charlotte," Mary said quietly. "You are not to blame. No one, really, is to blame."

"Except a road that came between neighbors," Charlotte answered, noting Mary's nod.

"The questions now are what is going to happen and what are we going to do?"

Buck sat down in a nearby chair. He was a large man with dark brown hair and a moustache. The chair looked a bit small for his height, but he sat comfortably. He looked at the women sitting near him. Mary was his heart and his children next. He downright hated to see her cry. And Charlotte was like a little sister to him, creating the same hurt for her. Reg was another matter. Reg was a hard man, nothing like his little sister who just happened to worship the ground her brothers walked on. So, he would have to help these two women so dear to him. Help them walk through this horrible tragedy and make sense of it.

"Charlotte, our boys will be okay. How's Milo?" Buck asked.

Mary's hand flew to her mouth. "Oh, Charlotte! I didn't even ask about Milo. I'm so sorry."

Charlotte made a sympathetic murmur. "It's alright, Mary. It's been quite a morning. He's sore and in some pain, Buck, but he's going to be okay."

Her brother-in-law nodded quietly, hands in pockets.

"Well, I had better be getting back," Charlotte stated in a flat voice. "No doubt the sheriff will be around."

Mary hugged her sister-in-law fiercely, then looked her straight in her blue eyes. "It's going to be alright, Charlotte. You'll see." Charlotte nodded before walking out the door.

Chapter 4

Milo gritted his teeth until the worst of the pain passed. His side hurt and so did his leg.

There were areas of red where the pellets had hit him. He didn't question his father and his decision to ride over to Mr. Wiggins's place. After all, Mr. Wiggins had lorded it over Papa that he was the one with the power to make Papa go out of his way to retrieve the water when necessary. They had a well, but it wasn't that deep and sometimes it went dry. In those times they had to ride over on the buckboard and bring water back.

Now, as he thought about Mr. Wiggins's death, Milo wished things had not turned out the way they did. Mr. Wiggins was a nice enough man when he wasn't being territorial about the creek. He hated to think how Mrs. Wiggins and her daughters would react to his death and to Papa's involvement.

Best avoid those thoughts right now. He had to get well. Papa needed him to help him on the farm. His older brothers could help out a few days. but they were married and already had a farm of their own to look after. Granted, Papa's was bigger, but all the farms required hard work. Milo had always been a little sickly as a child. Now that he was an adult (for that is what he saw himself as) he had not been too sick in a long while. And he did not want this to keep him down.

His thoughts turned to Lucy, his girlfriend. She was beautiful with her warm brown eyes, dark blonde hair and full red lips. He had met her at church. Lucy was a bit on the shy side at first, but soon came to be the sunny girl he loved. Loved. Gosh! Well, he thought, I guess I do love her. Milo smiled.

Chapter 5

Later in the day, Sheriff Wilson paid a visit to Reginald and Milo. He tied his horse to a hitching post. for he still preferred the horse to the new mechanical cars, walked to the front door and knocked. Reginald opened the door and brought it open wider when he saw it was the sheriff.

"Evening, Abram," Reginald said and gestured for him to come inside.

"Evening, Reg," he replied. Upon seeing Charlotte, he took off his hat and nodded. "Evening, Charlotte."

"Hello, Abram," she answered. "How is Polly?"

"She's doing fine, thank you. I'll tell her you asked after her."

"Please do," Charlotte said.

"Sit down, Abram," Reginald offered, pointing to the nicest padded chair.

Sheriff Wilson sat down in the comfortable chair. He took a moment to look at husband and wife, then spoke.

"Reginald, you know I'll have to charge you with Malcolm's death. And I'd be calling my lawyer if I were you."

"I'll answer the charge by saying it was self-defense," Reginald said.

Sheriff Wilson held up a hand. "Save that for the jury." He looked again at husband and wife. "Well, I reckon we need to be going," he said while standing to his full height. "Where's Milo?"

"He's in back. I'll get him," Reginald said. He came back in a few minutes with a pale Milo. Charlotte gave him a hug. Reginald looked at Charlotte, then walked to her. He put his hands on her arms and said, "We'll be back soon as we can." Charlotte nodded mutely, willing the tears not to fall. She just watched as the sheriff led her husband to jail.

Early the next morning, Charlotte's son, William, came by for a visit. He had heard what had happened. William looked much like his father with his dark hair and blue eyes. William had a bad ear infection as a child, leaving him with some hearing loss.

"Good morning, Mother," he said, hugging her. "How are you?"

"I'm going to be fine, William," she answered with a slightly raised voice. "I was wondering if you would do me a favor."

"Sure thing. What is it?" he asked.

"Would you take this check to the jail and pay your father's and Milo's bail?" she asked him.

William looked down at the check and back at his mother. She looked tired, he thought. Tired and worried. "I will." He was glad to see a little of the worry lift from her face.

William nodded and, "I'll come back this afternoon and help with the garden."

Charlotte looked even more relieved. "Thank you, William! We really appreciate that."

William hugged his mother once more and began his ride to town. Charlotte watched him go and was grateful he had offered to help with the garden. She wanted Milo to rest.

Chapter 6

William came back as he had promised. He helped his mother pick the peas that were ready to be harvested due to the warm weather. Afterwards, he went inside and had a cup of coffee with her.

"Mother," he began. "It's all going to work out in the end. I need to tell you, though, that the sheriff wouldn't accept the check for bail."

Charlotte put down her cup and looked at her son. "Why not?"

"The sheriff said because it was potentially a murder, he couldn't set bail. And the judge agreed with him," William answered.

Charlotte's frown lines were back. "Well, we'll just have to manage on our own right now."

"I know it's going to be alright, William," Charlotte said. "But it's going to be mighty hard to look Abigail in the eyes." She placed her coffee cup and saucer on the side table.

"What on earth possessed Malcolm to draw his weapon like that?"

William shook his head, looking down. "We might never know." With that, Charlotte nodded. She looked up at the door when she heard a sound. There was a knock on the door. William didn't hear it, so Charlotte went to answer the door. It was Mary.

"Mary! What are you doing out this time of evening?" Charlotte asked. She opened the door wider so her sister-in-law could come inside.

William saw his mother getting up and he had turned to the door. "Aunt Mary! It's nice to see you."

Mary hugged her nephew and, talking a little louder, told him, "It's good to see you, William. It's good for you to help your Mama." William nodded.

"Well, I reckon I'll go for now, Mother," he told Charlotte. "Let me know if you need anything." Charlotte nodded as she hugged her son good night.

She turned to Mary after William had left. "Come on and sit down. Do you want some coffee?"

Mary sat down and lifted her eyes to Charlotte. "That would be great."

After settling down again with fresh coffee for both of them, Mary explained why she was there. "Charlotte, I talked with Clayton this afternoon. He's as upset as the rest of us are. He'll be by tomorrow to check on you, but he wanted to go talk with Reginald first."

"That's fine," Charlotte answered. "I expected him to check on Reginald first." She looked down at her hands, then back at Mary. "Mary, what is going to happen to Abigail and the girls? I don't know if I can even face them right now."

Mary sighed. "From what I know, she and the girls are going to stay with her parents for now. I don't know what will become of the farm."

Charlotte looked at her best friend and said, "Why? Why did Reginald have to go over there today, of all days? Why couldn't he have just let it alone?"

"You know Reginald," Mary answered. "When he gets something on his mind, he's gonna do it or bust! Now, Clayton would have waited and weighed the matter." Mary spoke of her brother, Reginald's twin, Clayton.

Charlotte nodded. "I can appreciate that about Clayton. But I guess we'll have to wait and see what happens tomorrow."

The next day shone bright and cooler than the day before. It was as though the weather agreed that it should not be too hot for what was going on in the little community. The news of what had taken place spread far and wide, and very quickly. People could not believe what they were hearing. Malcolm Wiggins was dead, shot by Reginald Smith. But it was self-defense, they said. But Abigail did not believe it. She was sure her husband, her kind, sweet man, would not have drawn a weapon on their neighbor without provocation.

What was she to do now? She had to plan a burial far too soon for her Malcolm. The girls were too young to really understand that their daddy was never coming back to them. She would have to move in with her parents for now, if there weren't enough finances to cover the cost of living for a young widow and her family. She just did not know. Right now, it hurt too much to even contemplate a funeral.

While all of this was running through Abigail's mind, Reginald was talking with his attorney in the jail cell in Millen.

E.K. Miller sat in a chair in Reginald's cell with his client on the bunk. He held a black fountain pen in his hand, poised to write more if necessary. "Let's go through this once more," he said. Reginald sighed deeply, ran his hand over his face and through his hair. "Ed, we've been over it a dozen times it seems! I can't remember anything else."

Ed put the top on his fountain pen and closed his notebook. "Alright, Reginald. But if you think of anything

else, no matter how small, you let me know, you hear?"
Reginald nodded. With that, Ed picked up the chair and
replaced it by Deputy Sanders' desk. He nodded to the
deputy before leaving.

Deputy Sanders walked over to Reginald' cell and talked
with him. "Can I get you anything, Reginald?"

"Yeah, a glass of water would be good," Reginald
answered. Deputy Sanders returned with a cold glass of water
and handed it to the man behind the bars. "Thanks," he said.
Draining the glass, he handed it back to the deputy.

The days dragged on into weeks and the weeks into a
month, then two and three. There were times when Reginald
thought it was all just a bad dream he was in and couldn't get
out of. But when he looked around, he was reminded afresh
of where he was and why he was there. Charlotte and Mary
visited as often as they could. Clayton was so busy helping
plant Reginald's farm as well as his own that he didn't have
time to come in to see his brother. Reginald missed their talks

and the way they helped each other. Everyone knew Clayton was the kinder of the two.

He wanted to see Milo and his nephews, Michael and Barry. They could talk to each other through the bars and be heard four cells down. Reginald had apologized to them all for getting them into this. They were young men, though, and took being locked up with as much dignity and good nature as they could.

One afternoon Charlotte came into the sheriff's office with a smile on her face. Reginald could tell it was a pasted smile, but he appreciated her show of courage. She greeted the deputy and he pulled over the chair from beside his desk so she could sit comfortably. "Thank you, deputy," she smiled. After he had left the two to talk, Charlotte leaned forward and told Reginald what was on her mind.

"Reginald, the boys are helping as much as they can on the farm. And I appreciate them so much," she said. "The crops have been good to us and the garden even better.

William is taking everything to sell this morning and putting the rest of the grain in the bins."

Reginald smiled at his wife. He was truly blessed to have her. She had forgiven him for his affairs years ago with Dolly. He had a boy and a girl by her. It had taken Charlotte a while to come to terms with it, but she had, and he was eternally grateful.

"That's real good," he told her. "Thank them for me."

"I will," she answered. Charlotte looked at her husband critically. "You've lost weight. Do you want me to bring you food from home?"

"No," he shook his head. "I don't want you to go to all that trouble. Besides, it's not as safe for you or the children to travel at night. I'm doin' fine with this here food."

Charlotte stayed with him a few more minutes, then went around to see her son and her nephews. It had become a ritual now. Milo was glad to see his mother and he longed to go home. He had decided that he would never do anything wrong in his life ever again. The pain and discomfort he still had was wearing on him and he had lost weight as well. Michael and Barry were eagerly waiting for their mother and father to come see them. They, too, had decided it was not worth it to do anything unlawful. Charlotte finally had to say goodbye and was heading toward the door when a young boy came in followed by Sheriff Wilson.

The sheriff and Charlotte exchanged pleasantries, then he took the note the boy was so eager to give him. Sheriff Wilson opened it and read, then closed it. He nodded at the boy who then scampered off. Abram looked at Reginald then at Charlotte. "The bailiff says the jury selection starts in the morning at 9 o'clock. You won't be there, Reginald. The bailiff will let us know when the actual trial begins."

Charlotte was trembling ever so slightly. This was really the beginning of the end of this awful time in their lives. She would be so grateful when it was over. Not long, now, she told herself. With a nod, she turned and went out the door.

The next morning was cloudy and looked as though it would rain. Pretty soon there was no looking to it – it was raining. Good, thought Reginald. The crops are in and we'll be okay. By the end of the day the jury had finally been selected, Sheriff Wilson told him. It was not an easy feat, though, because so many people knew Reginald and Malcolm. Out of 120 men, they finally had twelve. At 5 o'clock the door of the sheriff's office opened again and it was the same young boy who had delivered the first message that morning. He quickly went to the Sheriff and handed him the note. Sheriff Wilson nodded at him and thanked him. The boy, knowing he was dismissed, quickly left the building. The sheriff opened the note and told Reginald, "The trial starts tomorrow morning. I best get word to Charlotte to bring your suit in." He went outside to give his deputy the word.

Chapter 7

The following morning, March 20, dawned bright after the previous afternoon's rain. There was still a chill in the air. Reginald' suit would keep him warm enough for the walk to the courthouse. As was protocol, he had to be in handcuffs. Milo, Michael, and Barry were with him. They all had their Sunday suits on and were in handcuffs as well. There were a few people on the streets, and they looked to see who was being escorted to the courthouse. There was a small intake of breath from a couple ladies, but Reginald held his head up. He walked beside Sheriff Wilson up the brick steps and into the courtroom. He looked around the courtroom, noticing all the people – people he knew, most of them family – in the pews. His eyes caught Charlotte's and she smiled encouragingly at him. The jury sat on the opposite side of the room. His attorneys were there waiting for him. He sat with them. The plaintiff's attorneys sat at a table across from him and his attorneys.

The judge was sitting in his chair at the front of the room. He knew Judge R.A. Lively as he had been in the courtroom many times as Justice of the Peace. Here, though, the judge did not look him in the eye but did look in his direction. The time had come for silence. The bailiff's voice was loud and clear as he said, "The Jenkins County Criminal Court will now come to order. Judge R.A. Lively presiding." Then he sat down.

"We are here," the judge began, "to find if these defendants are guilty of the murder of Malcolm Wiggins, allegedly committed this past December 25, 1921." He looked sternly over his reading glasses. "Is the state ready with the opening statement?"

Attorney R.E. Sanders stood and began his statement. "Yes, your honor. Gentlemen of the jury, it is my intent to prove that Reginald Smith, his son Milo and his nephews Michael and Barry did conspire to kill their neighbor Malcolm Wiggins. And on Christmas Day, no less." Mr. Sanders continued to outline the day in question, how

Reginald had his hired hands ride by Malcolm's house to see if he was home, and how he gathered three more people with him to commit his horrible deed. Malcolm Wiggins, Mr. Sanders continued, was inside his house when the Smiths began to fire upon his home, fatally wounding him. "So, you see, gentlemen of the jury, they must be held accountable for the death of Mr. Malcolm Wiggins. The state yields to the court, your honor."

E.K. Miller stood up and faced the judge then the jury. "Your honor. Gentlemen of the jury. Ladies and gentlemen. It is a fact that Mr. Malcolm Wiggins is dead. It is a fact that he was shot which led to his death. It is a fact that Mr. Reginald Smith and his son and nephews were riding in front of Mr. Wiggins' home on that fateful Christmas Day last year. It is a fact that Milo was driving the car that day. It is a fact that he was shot through the door of the car and injured. It is a fact that Milo never shot one of the guns." Mr. Miller paused for effect. "The only reason Reginald, Milo, Michael and Barry fired at all is because Mr. Wiggins fired first."

There was a murmur in the courtroom and the judge banged his gavel. Silence descended.

The attorneys for the state called over forty witnesses over the next two days to detract from the Smith's innocence. Consequently, their attorneys called more than forty witnesses over the next two days to claim their innocence. But the bombshell of the trial came two days after the beginning of it.

"Your honor," Mr. Daniels, a tall lanky attorney for Reginald stood before the judge. "If it please the court, I have asked Dr. Charles Martin to come here today and extract the Number 4 shot from Michael and Milo." There were several murmurings in the room and the jurists looked at each other then at the judge.

"This is most unusual, Mr. Daniels," the judge answered. "Do you feel it is necessary to help your case?"

"Yes, sir. And the fact that the young men in question need to have that buckshot out." He waited while the judge mulled it over. Mr. Sanders did not like the idea at all. "Your honor! This is highly irregular! In fact, I don't believe it has ever been done." The judge looked at both attorneys and said, "Very well, then."

A table was brought in with a white linen cloth over it. Dr. Charles Martin came in with his black medical bag. He was no nonsense today and quickly had a pillow under Michael's arm as he gave him a glass of water mixed with cocaine. It had been a while since cocaine started being used as an anesthetic. Within a couple minutes Michael's head slumped a bit. Dr. Martin leaned him back in the chair and, with his left arm propped up, began using his scalpel to cut into Michael's flesh. Some of the women in the audience gasped. He then used his forceps to take out the buckshot, Number 4, one by one. After each area he stitched up the small incisions and bandaged the arm well. Dr. Martin stood up, washed his hands then stretched his back as he dried his hands. He paused a moment.

Mr. Daniels took the opportunity to stand and explain why this was all necessary. "The buckshot wasn't taken out earlier because we wanted the jury to see that Michael was injured in his left arm. He could not handle the rifle much with that kind of injury. And we wanted to wait until today for Milo to have his buckshot taken out. Firstly, because he had to wait for the swelling to go down. Secondly, he could not have handled a gun at all since he was driving and was wounded by Mr. Wiggins." He turned to Dr. Martin. "Doctor, please continue."

Dr. Martin called Milo up to the table. He asked Milo to take off his shirt and pants. Milo looked at him astonished. Dr. Martin nodded encouragingly, and Milo did as he was asked. There were more gasps and Charlotte's face turned red, blushing enough for her son and her entire family.

"You can see, gentlemen of the jury," said Mr. Daniels, "that Milo has been shot with buckshot along his left arm, his left side, and his left thigh. And I'll wager that what the doctor takes out will be Number 4 buckshot, the same buckshot as was used in Malcolm Wiggins' shotgun."

Dr. Martin put another sheet over the right side of Milo and gave him a glass of water with cocaine mixed in it. Within a few minutes Milo was dozing comfortably. Dr. Martin began with his scalpel making small incisions along Milo's left arm and removing Number 4 buckshot. He continued down his side and into the upper thigh. It took him about an hour and a half to finish up with the stitching and bandaging. By that time, Milo was awake and sore but none the worse for wear. He took his seat again.

"Well, I think this court has had enough drama today," the judge said. "Court will recess until 9 o'clock in the morning. Attorneys, be prepared for closing arguments." He banged his gavel. Everyone waited until the judge had left the room before they began filing out. It seemed there was much to say about the day's events and small groups stood outside the courthouse conversing before going their separate ways. Inside the courtroom Reginald, Milo, Barry, and Michael lined up and were escorted back to the jail. They were allowed to change into their everyday clothes and have a meal. They talked to each other making sure Milo and Michael were as comfortable as they could be before they retired for the night. Reginald lay there for a long time contemplating the day's events.

It had been embarrassing for Milo to bare himself as he had. But he looked straight ahead and handled it like a man. Well, he was a man, wasn't he? Twenty years old now. How had that happened so quickly? Reginald wasn't much of a praying man, but he prayed now that the three young men would have a light sentence or no sentence at all. Tomorrow would be the fourth day of the trial.

The morning ushered in the fourth day of the trial. The judge had said he wanted the attorneys to give their closing arguments today. Reginald wondered what would be said. He quickly washed up then ate his breakfast, as did the other three. They all dressed in their suits and began the walk across to the courthouse. Once inside they sat at their table with their attorneys and waited. They did not have to wait long. Everyone was ordered to be quiet as the judge presided over the trial. Mr. Sanders was the first to utilize closing arguments.

"Gentlemen of the jury, it is my hope that we have given you the facts that maintain that Reginald Smith, his son Milo, his nephews Michael, and Barry Jenkins conspired to and did kill Malcolm Wiggins. They purposely drove over on Christmas Day of last year counting on Mr. Wiggins being in a vulnerable position because of the holiday. Once there they mercilessly opened fire upon Mr. Wiggins and shot him inside his own home, riddling the home with buckshot and bullets. The only recourse to this heinous crime is to return with a verdict of guilty. The state rests."

Mr. Miller stood and faced the jury. "Gentlemen of the jury. You have seen quite a lot and heard quite a lot during this trial. You have heard the facts that I stated at the beginning of the trial and have seen the Number 4 buckshot taken from the bodies of Michael Jenkins and Milo Smith. You have heard the testimony of the witnesses for the defendants and have heard their own testimonies. There was no conspiracy to commit murder. This was an accident that should never have taken place. No one was supposed to get hurt, much less die. It is my hope that you will use your common sense and return with a verdict of not guilty for the murder of Malcolm Wiggins. Thank you." With that he sat down.

"Gentlemen of the jury," the judge told them. "It is now time for you to go into the jury room and examine the case. Read over the notes, remember what witnesses have said, and come back with a verdict of guilty or not guilty." He banged his gavel. With that, the jurists got up and walked single file to the jury room and closed the door. It was 4:30 o'clock.

Back at the sheriff's office the defendants washed up and had their supper. They were quiet this evening, more so than other evenings. It was March 24th, and he was hoping that things would be back to normal – as much as normal could be now – within a day or two. Reginald drifted off to sleep.

Anxious to get to the courtroom the next morning, Reginald hurried through his morning routine. After breakfast he was ready to go and hear the response from the jury. Sheriff Wilson noticed Reginald' face and hid a smile. He hoped justice would be served and – secretly – he hoped they would be found not guilty.

After sitting down at the defendant's table Reginald whispered to Mr. Miller, "What do you think?" His attorney looked at him somberly. "I don't think anything at this point. Juries can be fickle." At that time the judge entered the courtroom, and everyone stood until he was seated. The jury looked uncomfortable but were dutifully there. The foreman was ready for his response.

"Gentlemen of the jury," the judge began. "Have you reached a verdict?" The foreman of the jury stood and told the judge, "No, your honor, we did not." The judge looked at them all with shock in his face. "And how's that?" The foreman answered, "It was 11-1 in favor of guilty." The judge thought a moment, running his hand over his bottom jaw. Finally, he said, "Very well. In that case I must find the case a mistrial." There were murmurings in the audience. The judge banged his gavel and asked for quiet.

"Mr. Sanders," the judge said. "Do you have further plans for these defendants?"

Mr. Sanders stood. "Yes, your honor. The state charges them with second degree murder."

"Seeing as how this trial ended in a mistrial, meaning the defendants are not charged with conspiracy to commit first degree murder, the state has charged them with second degree murder. Therefore, the defendants will be remanded to the county jail until the next trial. I would like to see both attorneys in my chambers to discuss change of venue." With that, the judge banged his gavel and was moving toward the door to his chambers.

Mr. Miller talked with Reginald, Milo, and the Jenkins brothers quickly. Now listen, that's a good sign that they did not convict you of first-degree murder. I've got to go talk with the judge right now, but I'll be over later to talk with y'all." With that he and the other attorneys were gone.

Reginald felt his head spin a bit. Hadn't they just found him not guilty? He should have been released, shouldn't he? His boys should have been released, shouldn't they? He looked at Sheriff Wilson with a bewildered look. The sheriff led them back to the county jail and into their cells. It was midafternoon, and the sun was beginning to go down. About an hour later, Mr. Miller came into sheriff's office.

After settling himself in a chair so he could look at all the defendants, he began. "Well, what happened over at the courthouse was a legal strategy. You all were acquitted by reason of a mistrial, meaning that all twelve of the jurors did not agree that you were guilty. But the state's attorneys believe you are guilty so they are trying you on the next crime in line – second-degree murder. That is what we begin working on now. And the judge has decided that the next trial will take place in Bulloch County."

"Why?" asked Milo.

"Because they had such a difficult time finding twelve jurors for this trial. So, they will go outside the county to find those jurors," Mr. Miller answered. "The judge will let us know when the next trial date is." Quiet in the sheriff's office. Mr. Miller broke the silence by saying, "Well, get some rest tonight. I'll be in touch." He nodded to the sheriff and deputy and walked out the door.

Chapter 8

Days seemed to run together, and Reginald had a difficult

time keeping up with the correct days. It helped to read the

newspaper every day, compliments of the sheriff. Charlotte

would come by and let him know what was going on at the

farm. Turned out his sons William and Lawrence, along with

Clayton, shouldered the main burden for his farm. But they

kept it running, for which he was extremely grateful.

Jeremiah did what he could, but Thomas still had not put in

his fair share of the work, which galled Reginald. Reginald

had long ago given Charlotte the right to write checks on his

account and she brought in the books from time to time for

him to look over. Things were tight, with the attorney fees

coming in now, but they were still making it.

March turned into April. One afternoon near the end of

April Mr. Miller came into the jail and stood before them all.

"Well, you will be transferred to the Bulloch County jail on

April 30 and the trial begins May 1st. I realize your families

may not be able to visit you as often but hopefully the trial will be over soon." He talked with them and answered their questions then left quietly. Reginald asked Deputy Sanders if he could get word to Charlotte regarding the upcoming events. The deputy said he would be glad to.

That afternoon Charlotte came into the jail. She had her smile on her red lips and Reginald noticed it even made it up to her pretty green eyes. He felt a wave of relief. Charlotte talked with Reginald first.

"How are you, Reginald?" she asked as she sat down in the chair Deputy Sanders provided for her.

"I'm alright," Reginald answered. "Ready to have this trial over with."

"I know you are," she said. "We're ready for it to be over, too." She paused then proceeded. "I miss you so much." Reginald looked at her and smiled. "I miss you, too, Charlotte." They talked a few more minutes, then Charlotte went to see Milo, then Barry and Michael. After a while, she made her goodbyes and left.

Two days later Reginald, Milo, Barry, and Michael were taken to Bulloch County, Georgia. They were taken to the jail while the jury selection was going on. What Reginald did not know at the time was that there were 150 veniremen selected to choose a jury. It took three hours for the jury to be selected. By 1 o'clock in the afternoon, the trial began.

Once again, there were many family members and friends in the audience of the courtroom. Judge H.B. Collins was presiding over the trial. A.S. Taylor was the solicitor general for the state. Reginald and the young men had the same attorneys that had been with them previously. The first witness was the father-in-law of Malcolm Wiggins. All total, there were 100 witnesses – about half for the defense and half for the state – who gave their testimonies. By May 3rd, Reginald' fate had been sealed as he was tried first. The jury entered the guilty verdict for murder! He was to be taken to the penitentiary in Atlanta for his remainder of his sentence.

Chapter 9

Reginald was shocked! He certainly did not expect this verdict. His eyes sought out Charlotte and he saw that she was softly weeping. The jury recommended mercy and in so doing sentenced Reginald to a lifetime of imprisonment. At least he did not get the death penalty, he thought. After a few words with his attorneys, he was allowed to sit in on the rest of the trial.

"The jury will now hear the testimony for and against Michael Jenkins, Barry Jenkins, and Milo Smith," Judge H.B. Collins said. "Mr. Taylor," the judge intoned. So, the trial began for the three young men. There were many witnesses for the prosecution and the defense. And by the 8th day, the verdicts were in.

"Michael Jenkins," the judge said. Michael stood up on trembling legs. His arm was fully healed by now. "You have waived formal indictment and pled guilty to voluntary manslaughter. It is the sentence of this court that you be taken to the jail at Bulloch County and remain until a guard from the penitentiary in Atlanta takes you to said prison. You will remain there not less than six years and no more than twelve years at hard labor." Michael was visibly shaken. He sat so his knees did not give out on him.

"Barry Jenkins," the judge continued. Barry stood up, trembling from head to foot. Since he knew his brother's fate, he was prepared for at least as much. "You have waived formal indictment and pled guilty to voluntary manslaughter. It is the sentence of this court that you be taken to the jail at Bulloch County and remain until a guard from the penitentiary in Atlanta takes you to said prison. You will remain not less than three years and not more than five years at hard labor." It was less than Michael! How had that happened? Whatever the reason he was thankful it was no more than five years.

"Milo Smith," the judge said. Milo stood up. He was healed from his wounds as well. He stood on trembling legs and faced the judge. "The jury has reached a verdict of not guilty. You are free to go." Milo could barely believe what he had just heard. He was free! Free to go home. He cried.

"Your honor, in the matter of Reginald Smith, we would like to seek a retrial," Mr. Miller said. "It has come to our attention that all the evidence has not been looked at. The car used that day has bullet holes that might shed some light on the actual course of events."

"This is highly remarkable, Mr. Miller." He considered a moment. "But the court will take it into consideration. For now, the defendants – save Mr. Milo Smith – will be returned to the Bulloch County jail then be taken to the Atlanta Penitentiary." The judge banged his gavel.

On the way back to the Bulloch County jail Reginald talked with Barry and Michael. He told them, again, how sorry he was to have involved them at all. They said that they were men now and knew the potential for something going wrong. "At least," Barry said, "There are limits for the time I'm there. That's one good thing." His brother knew he was grasping at straws to find the good somewhere. It had been a long day and they were all ready to eat supper and go to bed.

May 9th dawned cloudy and cool. Reginald has been doing a lot of thinking throughout the night and he had decided that he may as well get used to doing some physical labor, so he had started doing pushups. They would keep his body from wasting and he would be able to handle the physical labor better. He wasn't too old for the pushups. So, he did some in the morning and would do some at night.

It was a few days later that a guard from Atlanta came and took Reginald, Michael and Barry away. They were trying very hard to keep from crying. With luck, they would be back home in three to six years, which was still a long time.

Chapter 10

Reginald had been taken on the long trip to Atlanta and checked in with the others. The pen, as it was called, was a huge dark gray building that could house 3000 inmates. It was completed in 1902. Even though it was a medium-security prison, it was not for the faint of heart. Since Reginald was a farmer, it was decided he would help tend the crops. But he did not stay long. He was back in Bulloch County on July 5th.

On July 6th of 1922 the case was being retried in Bulloch County for Reginald. This was the third trial. They had begun the trial and included the car as evidence. But to see the evidence, the judge, jury, attorneys, and defendant had to go outside to see it. Well, this particular day, the twenty-sixth of July, Clayton had come to hear the proceedings. He wanted to see the car, too, so when they all filed out, he walked with them. Reginald decided to stay in the courtroom. No one seemed to notice the switch up. But Mr. Miller knew Reginald was staying in the courtroom.

The Model T had seen its better days. Shotgun pellet holes were all over the left side of the car. It certainly did put in perspective how much Malcolm Wiggins had shot at them and wounded three of them. On the way back Mr. Miller let it be known that Clayton was with them instead of Reginald. The judge was so shocked that he felt he had been purposefully cheated. He looked at Clayton again and could not see the difference between the two brothers. But when he reentered the courtroom, he saw Reginald sitting quietly in the same chair he was in before they left. This caused Judge Collins considerable ire. The judge was so upset that he stopped the trial and demanded the defendant be taken back to the pen. So, back to the pen Reginald went. Reginald noted that the judge banged his gavel twice.

Chapter 11

The weeks continued to turn into months and the months into another year. Mr. Miller sought a new trial for Reginald on the grounds that the defendant was entitled to being tried in his own hometown. The venue was denied but the trial was granted and kept in Bulloch County. This would actually be his third trial since Judge H.B. Collins had stopped the third trial.

On October 26, 1923, Reginald was sitting in the Bulloch County Courtroom. The attorneys had brought their witnesses and the jury had deliberated just over four hours. They now filed back into the courtroom and took their seats. The foreman handed the judge the sheet of paper with the verdict on it. The judge looked at it nodded his head and looked at Reginald.

"Mr. Smith, please rise," said the judge. He looked over his spectacles at Reginald and pronounced. "Mr. Smith, the jury has found you to be guilty of the murder of Malcolm Wiggins. You are hereby sentenced to the penitentiary in

Atlanta to serve out your life sentence at hard labor." The judge banged his gavel.

Mr. Miller actually looked downcast for a moment. Then he looked at Reginald and said, "We'll get something going again, Reginald."

"I don't know what else you can do, but I surely do appreciate your efforts," Reginald said. So, back to the pen he went.

One afternoon Mr. Miller came to see Reginald. "Reginald!" he almost shouted. "Reginald, we're going to get a new trial."

Reginald was a bit stunned. Had he heard right? "A new trial?" he asked.

"That's right," Mr. Miller said.

"How come?" asked Reginald.

"Because we learned after the trial that two of the jurors are related to Attorney Taylor. That's enough to get a new trial. I'm going over to see the judge as soon as I get back to Statesboro," said Mr. Miller.

"Alright. You know where to find me," Reginald quipped.

Mr. Miller did talk with Judge Collins. And the judge was not happy to know that two of his jurors were related to the prosecutor. So, with this in mind, he ordered a new trial. It was slow moving on the new trial. Jurors had to be selected again and the judge wanted to make sure there was no one related to either attorney or the defendant. It turned out that only 11 jurors were in the jury box. They could not find a twelfth juror, but both sides agreed to the 11.

This was the fourth trial beginning on July 30, 1924. Witnesses were heard from both the prosecution and the defense. It took only a couple days to have the jury go for deliberation. When the jury came back with the verdict, Reginald stood at Judge Collins's request.

"Mr. Smith, you have had witnesses appear here and give their testimonies. The jurors have listened to the evidence and examined it. Now the verdict is in. Mr. Smith, you are declared guilty of voluntary manslaughter. Your sentence is no less than 15 years and no more than 20 years at hard labor at the Atlanta Penitentiary." The judge banged the gavel.

On the 29th of October 1924, Reginald was once again in the defendant's seat in Bulloch County. Another trial, the fifth trial, had been convened and once again Reginald heard the testimonies from witnesses. He was not quite sure of the reason he got a fifth trial, but he was grateful for it. At least he got to see Charlotte and his children, Mary and Clayton and their families. Besides, there had been so many trials that he was losing count. He really did not want to go back to the penitentiary but if he had to, he had to. It had not been as bad on him as on some at the pen, but it was not home by any stretch of the imagination. He had learned to keep his mouth shut and do his job. When the jurors came out this time, things were a bit different. The foreman handed Judge Collins the verdict. The judge looked at it and, without any emotion, said, "Mr. Reginald Smith, you have been found guilty of voluntary manslaughter. The sentence is one to two years hard labor at the penitentiary in Atlanta." And he banged his gavel. The judge was a fair man, and it was a while before the guard from Atlanta could get back to pick up Reginald. So, Reginald was able to stay at the Bulloch County jail over the holidays. He was able to see his family and the friends who would drop by.

Reginald was brought back to the penitentiary in Atlanta on January 25th, 1925. He resumed his job of farmer and worked in the wood shop when there was nothing to do on the farm. He might continue doing the wood working after he was released. He seemed to have a knack for it. Charlotte was still making a go of the farm with the help of Clayton, William, and Lawrence. Even Jeremiah was helping more. Thomas still was not up to the task. His youngest, Minerva, was 14 now. Time had really passed by. It had been just over four years since that fateful day.

On January 24th, 1926, the warden called Reginald to his office. He had been pleased with Reginald's work ethic and the production he had put out. The warden's office was bigger than his cell and much more opulent. The warden was a fair man who truly wanted to rehabilitate the inmates, for those who did not have to serve a life sentence. He had heard Reginald's story and was drawn to him. It wasn't every day that a man was tried five times for the same offense, or close to it. But Reginald had survived.

"Reginald, have a seat," the warden offered. Reginald sat down in a chair opposite him. "The reason I asked you here, Reginald, is because it's time for you to go home and I wanted to be the one to tell you."

"Home?" Reginald asked with a croak. "Truly, sir?"

The warden smiled. "Truly. You've been a model prisoner and have served a year. You're being paroled, which means you must meet with a parole officer until the end of your sentence, which is in another year. Can you do that?"

"Yes, sir," answered Reginald. "I can do that, sir."

"Alright, then. Tomorrow you'll be going home. I wish every inmate was as honest and good as you," the warden told him.

"Thank you, sir," Reginald said. "I appreciate this very much."

"You're welcome. You've earned it." With that, the warden dismissed him, and he went back to his cell. Tomorrow couldn't come soon enough!

The next day brought out the sunshine. Reginald looked back at the pen once more before getting into the back seat of the guard's automobile. He would not have chosen this journey he had been on, but he had changed a bit while on it. The drive took them several hours to complete and the guard dropped Reginald off at the sheriff's office. He walked in.

Deputy Sanders looked up and broke into a grin. "Well, I swunee! Look who's here, Sheriff!" Sheriff Wilson came out of his office and looked Reginald up and down, then walked over to him and shook his hand. "Welcome back, Reg."

"Thank you, Abram," answered Reginald. "It's good to be back."

"I imagine you're ready to get yourself back home," said Abram.

"Yes, sir. That thought has crossed my mind," Reginald agreed.

"Well, come on. I'll take you to your house." So the two walked out to the sheriff's patrol car – for he now had a car – and Reginald went home.

Epilogue

On January 24th, 1926, Reginald was logged out of the Atlanta Penitentiary. He remained on parole until January 24th, 1927. His farm had flourished under the oversight of Charlotte and the family. He was ever so grateful he still had her by his side. Because of the mountain of legal fees, he had to sell off 619 acres of his land to pay debts and secure seed for the next planting season.

By the end of 1932 he was back on the jury list for Jenkins County, which gave him a new respect for the position of juror, and he was active again in the community. It was the same year he lost his beloved Milo to pneumonia. Reginald was a resilient man who was hard on people when he needed to be. But he also had learned a little humility and compassion which Charlotte had noticed. On February 10th, 1950, Reginald passed away after an illness of several months. In his will, he left his son, Thomas, $1.

Made in the USA
Columbia, SC
11 August 2024

40332421R00052